PEOPLE OF PRIDE

25 Great LGBTQ Americans

by Chase Clemesha, MD

CAPSTONE EDITIONS

a capstone imprint

To my parents for their endless support—CC

People of Pride is published by Capstone Editions, an imprint of Capstone.
1710 Roe Crest Drive
North Mankato, Minnesota 56003
www.capstonepub.com

Library of Congress Cataloging-in-Publication Data is available on the Library of Congress website.
ISBN: 978-1-68446-216-2 (hardcover)
ISBN: 978-1-68446-217-9 (ebook PDF)

Summary: What do Frank Ocean, Ellen DeGeneres, George Takei, and Sharice Davids have in common? They're all proud LGBTQ Americans. Featuring people from a variety of occupations and backgrounds, this collection of 25 short biographies demonstrates the diversity, accomplishments, and pride of the American LGBTQ community.

Image Credits
AP Photo: Marcio Jose Sanchez, 37; Courtesy of the Family of Neena Schwartz: 51; Getty Images: Bettmann, 57, Brownie Harris, 11, 55, Dimitrios Kambouris, 19 left, Donna Ward, 9, Focus on Sport, 17, Frederick M. Brown, 19 right, General Photographic Agency, 35, Ilya S. Savenok, 31, Jack Vartoogian, 21, James Keyser/The LIFE Images Collection, 27, Melchior DiGiacomo/Sports Illustrated, 43, Michael Brochstein/SOPA Images, 33, Mike Windle, 49, MPI, 39, ROBYN BECK, 25, Suzi Pratt/FilmMagic, 41; Library of Congress Prints and Photographs Division; 15, 47; Shutterstock: Featureflash Photo Agency, 53, John Gress Media Inc, 45, s_bukley, 13; Wikimedia: NARA, 23, U.S. National Library of Medicine, 29

Design Elements
Shutterstock: Amma Shams, ARTvektor, Benjavisa Ruangvaree Art, Dinara May, kasha_malasha, Markovka, Naatali, Natasha Pankina, Natewimon Nantiwat, Neti.OneLove, Orfeev, samui, SonyaDehartDesign.com

Designed by Sarah Bennett

All internet sites appearing in the back matter were available and accurate when this book was sent to press.

Printed in China

Table of Contents

Growing Up Gay

Growing up, I never really felt I was all that different from any other kid, but being gay added an extra layer of uncertainty. There was always a concern that people wouldn't accept me. From making friends to finding a career path, growing up can be hard. Anything that makes someone feel the slightest bit different can make it even harder.

Being gay never defined me, and it never defined what I could be. I took pride in my success in the sciences as well as performing in theater and ballet. My parents taught me that I could do anything I put my mind to. If I wanted to help teach a complex science class, I knew I could. If I wanted to perform in *The Nutcracker* ballet, I knew I could. Being gay never limited what I could do. It was just a part of me. A part that I'm proud of.

It's important that young people have role models to look up to—especially people who are like them. When I was young, I always wished there were more well-known LGBTQ role models, specifically in science and medicine. I decided to become a doctor partly because I wanted to support LGBTQ patients by providing sensitive care. I also wanted to help show young, aspiring scientists that they belong in medicine if that's where their passion lies.

The incredible people in this book have done outstanding things in their fields, from music and art to science, sports, medicine, and more. They all have so much to be proud of. Today, it's wonderful to see more open and proud LGBTQ people in the media than ever before. But I feel it would be great if there were even more diverse role models to look up to in a variety of other careers.

Writing *People of Pride* is a way for me to show all young people some of the great contributions LGBTQ individuals have made. I want to show young people that they can decide who and what they're going to be. If you are part of the LGBTQ community, it is a beautiful part of who you are, but it is only one part. You get to be proud of who you are—your whole self. And you get to be proud of the good things you do, whatever they are. Just like the people celebrated in this book.

• • • • *Chase*

Introduction

This book is a rainbow of biographies.
Here are 25 (and more) lesbian,
gay, bisexual, or transgender people
who accomplished great things,
all together in one book!

These LGBTQ people are in the arts,
literature, entertainment, science, medicine,
sports, politics, advocacy, and business.
In other words, the full, diverse range of
occupations and interests that all people pursue.

These people's worlds are all different.
Each of their struggles is different.
They've achieved different goals. But they
all worked hard and, in spite of challenges,
they succeeded. Their inspiring journeys
are all something to be proud of!

Wanda Sykes (1964–) is an actor, writer, and comedian known for her sense of humor and bubbly personality. After college, she worked for the U.S. government with a top security clearance. After a few years, she knew this wasn't the right job for her. Sykes loved to make people laugh, and friends often told her, "You should be on the stage!" So she began performing at local clubs. Sykes loved it, and the audiences loved her too. She has now appeared in many movies and TV shows and has won awards for her writing and performances. Sykes charms audiences with jokes about herself, her family, and politics.

Wanda Sykes is proud of being able to help people have fun laughing at life.

When he was young, **Andy Warhol** (1928–1987) sometimes felt like he didn't fit in. He also had health problems that often kept him home from school. But like his mother, Warhol was good at drawing. Even though his parents didn't have much money, they bought him a camera and signed him up for art classes. Warhol liked expressing himself through lines, shapes, and color, and he went on to study art in college. Warhol became well known for his colorful paintings of soup cans and celebrities, and he helped lead the Pop Art movement of the 1950s and '60s. He said, "In the future, everyone will be world famous for 15 minutes."

Andy Warhol was **proud** of his **art,**

which made him **world famous**

well beyond 15 minutes.

During World War II, when **George Takei** (1937–) was young, he and his family were forced out of their home in Los Angeles, California. They were sent to internment camps along with many other Japanese Americans. Japan was an enemy in the war, and the U.S. government became distrustful of Americans with Japanese heritage, imprisoning them in camps around the country. As he grew up, Takei never forgot how hard that was for his family.

It became Takei's mission in life to raise awareness of "that dark and shameful chapter of American history." As an adult, he started acting and became a well-known actor on the TV show *Star Trek*. In addition to acting, Takei has written plays and books. He is also an advocate for justice. He has spoken out in favor of marriage equality for all and highlighted the struggles of Japanese Americans. Takei is also known to millions of social media followers for his clever sense of humor.

George Takei proudly uses his fame to bring attention to the Prejudices that many people face.

Bayard Rustin (1912–1987) grew up as a Quaker, a type of Christianity in which people work for peace and justice. He was a natural leader and became involved in many causes, including the desegregation of buses, fair employment laws, and rights for Japanese Americans during World War II. Rustin believed in nonviolence. During that war, he spent more than two years in prison as a conscientious objector, refusing to be forced to fight. He said that peace was the best way to fight hate, and he shared these ideas with Martin Luther King Jr. But even within the civil rights movement, Rustin faced discrimination as a gay man. He often had to work behind the scenes, including when he organized the March on Washington in 1963, where Dr. King gave his famous "I Have a Dream" speech.

Bayard Rustin must have been very **proud** when 250,000 people came to Washington, D.C., to **peacefully** demand their **rights**.

Greg Louganis (1960–) loves to perform and compete. As a child, he took dance and gymnastics lessons. Then, at the age of nine, he began diving. Louganis loved bouncing off the diving board, sailing through the air, and gliding into the water. He worked hard to master the grace and skill needed to win trophies. He won medals in the 1976, 1984, and 1988 Olympic Games, and he also won six World Diving Champion titles. In the middle of his career, Louganis had the extra burden of staying healthy as an athlete with human immunodeficiency virus (HIV), the illness that causes acquired immunodeficiency syndrome (AIDS). He is one of the greatest divers in history.

Greg Louganis was proud to earn four **Olympic** gold medals and to be a **role model** for all athletes.

Lights! Camera! Action! Sisters **Lana** (1965–) and **Lilly Wachowski** (1967–) are American film writers and directors. They are also transgender women. Today, they know all about the glamour and action of Hollywood, but they didn't always. They grew up in the Chicago area, and as children, they enjoyed drawing and writing comics and going to the movies. Later, the Wachowskis started a painting and construction business. But they kept writing stories. They describe their relationship as kind and supportive. People who have worked with the Wachowskis say it's like they have "two bodies and one brain." The sisters are best known for writing and directing the popular science-fiction movie *The Matrix* and its sequels.

Lana and **Lilly Wachowski** are **proud** of their **teamwork** and their **successful filmmaking** careers.

Lana

Lilly

glaad

Alvin Ailey (1931–1989) was a dancer, choreographer, and founder of one of the most successful American dance companies. Raised by a single mother during the Great Depression, Ailey had a hard childhood. He was sometimes left with relatives while his mother looked for work. Ailey was introduced to dance in high school and fell in love with it. When he was 18, he started to become serious about professional dance. As his career progressed, Ailey started his own dance company and dance school. The Alvin Ailey American Dance Theater gave Black dancers more opportunities to perform, and it brought together ballet, modern, and jazz styles. Ailey united audiences of all races by showing Black heritage and culture in dance.

Alvin Ailey was proud of building an inclusive dance company that performed his artistic creations.

When **Sally Ride** (1951–2012) was in college, she was excited to read that NASA (National Aeronautics and Space Administration) was going to finally train women, as well as men, to be astronauts. More than 8,000 people applied for the job. Ride was one of the few chosen. She trained and worked hard at NASA for five years. Finally, she was picked to become the first American woman in space. Ride flew into space twice, where she had the important job of operating the shuttle's robotic arm to help release satellites. She also went on spacewalks and conducted scientific experiments. After she left NASA, she became a teacher. Ride loved getting young people interested in science and space.

Sally Ride was proud to have been a team member in America's space program.

Jeanne Córdova (1948–2016) grew up in a household with 11 brothers and sisters. She was a leader in her family—she made sure her younger siblings agreed on what TV shows to watch and that they finished eating their vegetables. After high school, Córdova thought she would become a nun or a social worker. But she found her real calling fighting for lesbians' rights and dignity. Córdova said, "We're no longer going to be invisible." She took her leadership skills from childhood and put them to use. Córdova formed lesbian organizations and conferences. She fought against laws that were unfair to LGBTQ people. She also started a magazine for lesbians. She said her work as an activist was a "wild joyous ride."

Jeanne Córdova was proud of her work fighting for equality.

Jeanne
Córdova

As a child, **Maurice Sendak** (1928–2012) loved to read books, watch Mickey Mouse cartoons, and listen to his father tell exciting tales. Stories took him away from his own life and gave him wonderful new worlds to imagine. As he got older, Sendak also loved drawing these magical places. He filled his pictures with humor and charm, as well as drama and honest emotion. He said, "I refuse to lie to children." When his book *Where the Wild Things Are* was published, it won the Caldecott Medal, the top award for children's book illustrators. Later, it was made into a Hollywood movie. Sendak became one of the most popular children's book creators in the world.

Maurice Sendak was proud of making beautiful books that children and adults loved.

Friends and family told Sara Josephine Baker (1873–1945) that being a doctor wasn't the right thing for a "proper" young lady to do. That made her want to do it even more, especially because she was mourning her father and brother, who had recently become sick and died. So Baker went to one of the few medical schools willing to train women, the Women's Medical College of the New York Infirmary.

Baker became "Dr. Joe" and took a job with the city of New York. There, she cared for people in poor, crowded neighborhoods, where many babies were dying from a lack of proper health care. Baker realized that the most important thing was preventing babies and people from getting sick—rather than having to cure them after they became sick. She started programs to send nurses to teach mothers how to care for their new babies and keep them healthy. Baker's programs soon spread to other cities.

Sara Josephine Baker was proud

that her public health work

saved thousands of children's lives.

Frank Ocean (1987–) grew up in New Orleans, Louisiana, a city known for its music culture. He saw live jazz performances and listened to R&B songs with his mother. Ocean said, "Singing along with the radio became me wanting to be on radio." He wanted to make money as a musician, so he started recording songs by the time he was 13. When Ocean was still a teenager, Hurricane Katrina devastated New Orleans. He lost his music equipment in the disaster. But he kept working. He began to write songs for other musicians. Then, once he began to release his own music, his career grew quickly. Ocean's music blends hip-hop, soul, and jazz in a unique way. He has won Grammy awards and fame for his popular songs.

Frank Ocean is proud of the music he has created and the success his work has earned.

Even as a child, **Sharice Davids** (1980–) always seemed to have confidence in herself. As an adult, competing in mixed martial arts (MMA) increased her confidence even more. She said that MMA "made me a more solid, disciplined person, and it definitely helped with my mental toughness." Davids went to college in Kansas, then attended law school in New York. After graduating, she worked in a law firm and in government. Davids wanted to do more to serve her Ho-Chunk American Indian community and the people of Kansas, so she decided to run for Congress in 2018. It was a tough race, but she was up to the challenge—she won!

Sharice Davids is proud to be one of the first two American Indian women elected to Congress.

Helping out in his parents' hat shop after school, **Adrian Greenburg** (1903–1959) learned about clothes and fashion. He liked to draw, so he went to art school after graduating high school. One summer, Greenburg got a job designing costumes for a small theater. He found that he had a talent for creating beautiful clothes for stage characters. Soon he was working in Hollywood, designing costumes for the movies. Greenburg's most famous costumes were for the characters in *The Wizard of Oz*, including Dorothy's famous ruby slippers. Greenburg worked on more than 200 films during his career, and millions of people saw the elegant clothes and shoes he designed.

Adrian Greenburg was proud that his talent helped make great movies even better.

Ben Barres (1954–2017) had a girl's body when he was born. But as he grew, he felt like he was really a boy. It was confusing to him, and he hid those feelings. He grew up as a tomboy named Barbara who loved roughhousing, trucks, and science. Barres was an excellent student who went to medical school and began doing research on the brain. At age 40, Barres finally felt like his true self when he began transitioning from female to male. He was a world expert on brain cells and became the head of neurobiology at Stanford University. Barres earned the high honor of being elected to the National Academy of Sciences. He strongly supported women in the sciences and guided many young people into new areas of research.

Ben Barres took pride in his own discoveries and in the many young scientists he trained.

As a boy, **Leonard Bernstein** (1918–1990) loved music. When a relative gave his family an old piano, "Lenny" ran his fingers up and down the keys. It sounded wonderful to him. He spent hours practicing, and he learned to play beautiful melodies. His music filled their home. Bernstein wanted to fill his whole life with music, so he kept playing. He went on to write great songs, symphonies, a movie score, and the music for the Broadway hit *West Side Story*. His works have been enjoyed by millions of people. Throughout his career, Bernstein had a wide range of successes, including being the musical director of the New York Philharmonic Orchestra and winning a Grammy Lifetime Achievement Award.

Leonard Bernstein traveled the world to perform, lead orchestras, and teach, proudly sharing his love of music.

Mary Yu's (1957–) parents were immigrants who had to work low-wage jobs. They encouraged their daughter to get a good education and achieve higher goals. Yu's goal was soon clear—she wanted to help people. She worked for the Catholic Church for 10 years, trying to solve the problems of poverty and injustice. To do more, she set new goals and went to law school. Yu spent many years as a prosecutor and then as a judge. She oversaw all kinds of legal cases as well as hundreds of same-sex adoptions and marriages. When she was appointed as a justice of the Washington State Supreme Court, she became the first LGBTQ person to serve there. Yu believes that "we are really one human community, that we have more in common than we have differences."

Mary Yu is proud of her life's work to treat people with compassion and fairness.

Billie Jean King (1943–) loved sports, just like the rest of her family. When she was 11, she began learning to play tennis at the public courts near her home. It was fun, and she wanted to hit perfect shots. King practiced long hours to grow stronger and quicker. As a teenager, she began entering tournaments. Soon she was winning them. King became a world champion, winning dozens of major tennis tournaments, including 20 Wimbledon titles. Not only was she tough when playing tennis, but she was also tough when it came to fighting for women's rights. King wanted the same fair rules for everyone— in sports and in life. In the world of tennis, she fought for female players to get the same amount of prize money as male players.

Billie Jean King was especially proud of her work to create equal opportunities for women.

Even in high school, **Tim Cook** (1960–) was such a hard worker that his classmates voted him "Most Studious." His drive continued as he studied engineering and business and worked in technology companies. He joined Apple, a company now known around the world for making phones and computers. Since Cook has taken over as the chief executive officer (CEO) of Apple, the company has grown and created new products. Cook was the first major business leader to come out as gay. He is a very private person, but he knows young LGBTQ people need role models in all professions. He said that if hearing that the CEO of Apple was gay could help someone struggling to come to terms with who he or she is, then it was worth it.

Tim Cook is proud of his work as an innovator in the tech field and of being an openly gay CEO.

Jane Addams (1860–1935) grew up knowing she was fortunate. Her family had a lovely home, plenty of food, and lots of friends in their town. Unlike most women at the time, Addams was even able to go to college because of her family's wealth. After college, while she was traveling with a friend, Addams saw great hunger and poverty. She wanted to find a way to help. Back home in Chicago, Addams and her friend opened Hull House, a place for poor people to get food, childcare, job training, and even take art classes. Addams also worked to help pass laws to protect workers and children. Later, she spoke out against wars. She founded the Women's Peace Party, and she joined women around the world to work for peace.

Jane Addams must have been proud when she became the first American woman to be awarded the Nobel Peace Prize.

Ricky Martin (1971–) was a young boy in Puerto Rico when he began performing in TV commercials. At the age of 12, he joined the boy band Menudo and toured the world singing and dancing for thousands of people. Today, many consider him the "King of Latin Pop." He's known for his upbeat music and high-energy performances. Martin has sold millions of albums, bringing Spanish-language music to wider audiences. He has also used his fame to support organizations fighting for the well-being and rights of children. Martin served as a Goodwill Ambassador for UNICEF, an agency that provides help to children. He was inspired to start his own foundation after meeting poor children around the world.

Ricky Martin is proud to be a performer who brings joy to people through his music and charitable work.

In college, **Neena Schwartz** (1926–2018) was fascinated with how the human body works. She wanted to learn more about hormones and how they act as messengers to tell organs, such as the heart and brain, to do their jobs. Schwartz researched hormones to understand more about reproduction. Her discoveries had a groundbreaking impact on the field of medicine. Schwartz also started the Association of Women in Science, an organization that opened up more opportunities for women. When speaking about science, she said, "We must encourage women and other previously excluded groups to engage in it."

In her book, A LAB OF MY OWN,

Neena Schwartz told the world

about her work and how proud she was

to be a successful lesbian scientist.

Ellen DeGeneres (1958–) always loved to joke around. She became a comedian and then a TV sitcom star. When DeGeneres bravely came out as a lesbian on her show *Ellen*, many of her fans were shocked. Her show was canceled soon after. She wasn't offered any work for three years. But, much like Dory, the famous fish character DeGeneres voiced in the movies *Finding Nemo* and *Finding Dory*, DeGeneres just kept swimming. Because of her warm and fun personality and her persistence, she got the chance to start her own TV talk show, *The Ellen DeGeneres Show*. People loved seeing her on TV again, and she became an even bigger success.

Ellen DeGeneres is proud to be a pioneer for LGBTQ people in entertainment.

James Baldwin (1924–1987) was the oldest child in a large, poor family in Harlem, New York. At home, Baldwin's stepfather was hard on him and called him cruel names. Out in the world, Baldwin had to face prejudice against both Black Americans and gay people. But he knew he was smart, and he felt he had important things to say, so he began to write. He wrote stories and novels about the pain of being treated badly. Baldwin's stories even had gay and bisexual characters, which was unusual for books at that time. He wrote essays advocating for fairness and went on tours to speak about the Civil Rights Movement. His books became world famous.

James Baldwin was proud to be a voice fighting for the respect that he knew all people deserved.

Harvey Milk (1930–1978) loved talking and laughing with customers at his small camera shop in San Francisco, California. He also loved bringing his neighbors together to improve their community. Many LGBTQ people lived there, but they were often treated unfairly. Milk wanted to enter politics so he could do even more to help make things better. But he found out it wasn't so easy. He lost three elections. Still, Milk had lots of energy and hope. Finally, he became a San Francisco supervisor. Milk was one of the first openly gay people elected to office in the United States. He worked with his fellow supervisors to pass a law to stop discrimination against all LGBTQ people in San Francisco.

Harvey Milk was proud of bringing people together to fight for fairness.

More Outstanding LGBTQ People

Alison Bechdel (1960–) is a writer and illustrator of comics that focus on lesbian life and family relationships. She says her work is an ongoing project to show that "Queer lives have value. Not just to the people living them but to everyone."

Dan Choi (1981–) is a West Point graduate and former U.S. Army first lieutenant who challenged the military's "don't ask, don't tell" policy. He spoke out for the rights of all LGBTQ people to serve openly in the military.

Ruth Gates (1962–2018) grew up watching TV shows about the ocean, and she studied to be a marine biologist. She worked hard to try to find ways to save coral reefs dying from climate change and pollution.

Lorraine Hansberry (1930–1965) was the first Black female playwright to have play on Broadway. Her most famous work is *A Raisin in the Sun.*

Kathy Kozachenko (1954–) was elected to the Ann Arbor, Michigan, city council in 1974. She was the first openly LGBTQ person elected to a political office in the United States.

Martin Lo (1953–) is a scientist with NASA's Jet Propulsion Laboratory. He discovered the Interplanetary Superhighway, a vast system of gravity-based tunnels and passageways in the solar system that will make future space travel easier.

Audre Lorde (1934–1992) was a writer who used her poems "to speak the truth as I see it" and express deep emotions. She was proud that her work was read and that she was recognized for her powerful writer's voice.

Nergis Mavalvala (1968–) always liked math and science as a child. She became an astrophysicist studying space and time. Among many other honors, she was recognized as the LGBTQ Scientist of the Year in 2014.

Niki Nakayama (1975–) is a nationally recognized chef with a passion for traditional Japanese food. She has created her own top restaurant with 13-course dinners made from fresh, local ingredients.

Danica Roem (1984–) became interested in politics while working as a newspaper journalist. She was the first openly transgender person to be elected to any U.S. state legislature.

Jock Soto (1965–) had dreamed of being a professional dancer since he was five years old. At age 13, he left his Navajo Nation home to study ballet in New York. His dream came true when he grew up to become a principal dancer with the New York City Ballet.

Amandla Stenberg (1998–) is a film actor who is known for her roles in *The Hunger Games* and *The Hate U Give*. She has been an outspoken activist on social issues.

Walt Whitman (1819–1892) created new styles of poetry. He worked for decades on his collection of poems, *Leaves of Grass,* and is considered one of the most important American writers.

Jacqueline Woodson (1963–) is an author of many children's and adult books. She has won numerous awards, including the Newbery Medal and The Hans Christian Andersen Award, the highest international award for lifelong achievement.

Timeline of U.S. LGBTQ History

1924 The first gay rights organization in the United States, the Society for Human Rights, is founded.

1953 President Dwight D. Eisenhower signs Executive Order 10450, barring LGBTQ people from working in the federal government and military.

1955 Daughters of Bilitis is founded as the first U.S. lesbian rights organization.

1962 Illinois becomes the first state to make gay relationships not a crime.

1969 Police attempt to raid the Stonewall Inn bar in New York City, leading to several days of riots. These events are said to have energized the LGBTQ rights movement.

1973 *Homosexuality* is removed as a mental illness by the American Psychiatric Association.

1974 Kathy Kozachenko becomes the first openly LGBTQ person to be elected to a public office in the United States.

1977 Harvey Milk is elected to San Francisco's Board of Supervisors, where he introduces employment protections for gay and lesbian people. A year later, Milk is assassinated by a former Board member.

1979 About 100,000 people gather to demand equal civil rights at the National March on Washington for Lesbian and Gay Rights.

1993 "Don't ask, don't tell" is implemented in the military, forbidding LGBTQ people to serve openly.

1996 The Defense of Marriage Act is signed into federal law, stating that marriage is only between a man and a woman.

2000 Vermont legalizes same-sex unions.

2004 Massachusetts becomes the first state to legalize same-sex marriage.

2008 California passes Proposition 8, banning same-sex marriages in the state. Its passing begins the NOH8 campaign to advocate for marriage equality.

2015 The United States Supreme Court legalizes same-sex marriage in all 50 states.

2020 The U.S. Supreme Court rules to protect LGBTQ people from workplace discrimination on the grounds of their sexuality or gender identity.

Glossary of LGBTQ Terms

bisexual—being attracted to men and women

come out—to tell people you are LGBTQ for the first time

don't ask, don't tell—the military ban against LGBTQ people serving openly

gender—a person's feeling inside of being a male, female, somewhere in between, or neither; it can be the same, or different, from the sex assigned at birth

homosexuality—attraction to others of one's same sex

lesbian—a woman who is attracted to other women

LGBTQ—an acronym for lesbian, gay, bisexual, transgender, and queer; the Q can also stand for questioning one's sexuality

marriage equality—same-sex couples having the same right to get married as opposite-sex couples have

openly LGBTQ—a person who shares being LGBTQ with friends, family, and coworkers

queer—a term people use to express fluid identities and orientations

same-sex adoption—same-sex couples adopting children the same way opposite-sex couples do

transgender—gender identity being different from the cultural expectations of the sex assigned at birth

Source Notes

p. 10, "In the future…" Josh Tyrangiel, "Andy Was Right," *Time*, December 25, 2006, content.time.com/time/magazine/article/0,9171,1570780,00.html

p. 12, "that dark and shameful chapter…" Mike Dow, "'This Is My Legacy Project'—George Takei Talks 'Allegiance,'" *The Maine Edge*, December 19, 2018, themaineedge.com/style/this-is-my-legacy-project-george-takei-talks-allegiance

p. 18, "two bodies and one brain" Aleksandar Hemon, "Beyond the Matrix," *The New Yorker*, September 3, 2012, newyorker.com/magazine/2012/09/10/beyond-the-matrix

p. 24, "We're no longer going to be invisible" Hailey Branson-Potts, "Jeanne Córdova Dies at 67," *Los Angeles Times*, January 15, 2016, latimes.com/local/obituaries/la-me-jeanne-cordova-20160115-story.html

p. 24, "wild joyous ride" Riese, "Jeanne Córdova, Pioneering Lesbian Activist & Author, Dies," *The Pride*, January 24, 2016, thepridela.com/2016/01/jeanne-cordova-pioneering-lesbian-activist-author-dies/

p. 26, "I refuse to lie to children" Emma Brockes, "Maurice Sendak: 'I Refuse to Lie to Children,'" *The Guardian*, October 2, 2011, theguardian.com/books/2011/oct/02/maurice-sendak-interview

p . 30, "Singing along with the radio…" Amy Wallace, "Frank Ocean GQ Man Of The Year Interview," Genius, Nd, genius.com/Frank-ocean-frank-ocean-gq-man-of-the-year-interview-annotated

p. 32, "made me a more solid, disciplined person…" "Trailblazing Out Lawmaker Sharice Davids Takes on Inequality," NBC News, June 13, 2019, nbcnews.com/video/trailblazing-out-lawmaker-sharice-davids-takes-on-inequality-61840453720

p. 40, "we are really one human…" "Washington State Supreme Court Justice Mary Yu, Welcome Address," Central Washington University, October 16, 2015, youtube.com/watch?v=-DQKuQE4a3k

p. 48, "King of Latin pop" Hughes Nelson, "King of Latin Pop Artist Ricky Martin's video 'Tiburones,'" *Daily Music Roll*, January 31, 2020, dailymusicroll.com/video/king-of-latin-pop-artist-ricky-martins-video-tiburones.html

p. 50, "We must encourage women…" Neena B. Schwartz. *A Lab of My Own*. Amsterdam; New York: Rodopi, 2010, p. 1 of preface.

p. 58, "Queer lives have value…" "Queers & Comics Keynote: Alison Bechdel," The Graduate Center, CUNY, June 23, 2015, youtube.com/watch?v=kQrKPmnrZYw

p. 58, "to speak the truth…" Celia Fernandez, "12 Audre Lorde Quotes That'll Spark Conversation," *The Oprah Magazine*, January 8, 2019, oprahmag.com/life/relationships-love/g25776736/audre-lorde-quotes/?slide=8

All websites accessed on June 24, 2020.

Internet Sites

To learn more, or if you or someone you know needs support, help can be found at these sites.

Human Rights Campaign
hrc.org/

LGBTQ Youth Resources
cdc.gov/lgbthealth/youth-resources.htm

The Trevor Project
thetrevorproject.org/resources/

About the Author

Chase Clemesha, MD, grew up in California, where he enjoyed going to theme parks, running, studying science, and cooking. He has a Bachelor of Science degree in biology from the University of California San Diego and a medical degree from the University of Southern California, where he was elected to a national medical honor society.

Chase now lives in Florida and is continuing his training as an emergency medicine doctor. When he is not treating patients in the emergency room, he still enjoys visiting theme parks.